SandCastle

Sight Words

When Can You Play Again?

Kelly Doudna

Consulting Editor Monica Marx, M.A./Reading Specialist

Published by SandCastle™, an imprint of ABDO Publishing Company, 4940 Viking Drive, Edina, Minnesota 55435.

Printed in the United States.

Credits
Edited by: Pam Price
Curriculum Coordinator: Nancy Tuminelly
Cover and Interior Design and Production: Mighty Media
Photo Credits: Brand X Pictures, Corbis Images, Digital Vision, PhotoDisc, Stockbyte

Library of Congress Cataloging-in-Publication Data

Doudna, Kelly, 1963-
        When can you play again? / Kelly Doudna.
            p. cm. -- (Sight words)
        Includes index.
        Summary: Uses simple sentences, photographs, and a brief story to introduce six different words: again, had, his, me, when, your.
        ISBN 1-59197-478-X
        1. Readers (Primary) 2. Vocabulary--Juvenile literature. [1. Reading.] I. Title. II. Series.

PE1119.D68666 2003
428.1--dc21

                                                                        2003050322

SandCastle™ books are created by a professional team of educators, reading specialists, and content developers around five essential components that include phonemic awareness, phonics, vocabulary, text comprehension, and fluency. All books are written, reviewed, and leveled for guided reading, early intervention reading, and Accelerated Reader® programs and designed for use in shared, guided, and independent reading and writing activities to support a balanced approach to literacy instruction.

Let Us Know

After reading the book, SandCastle would like you to tell us your stories about reading. What is your favorite page? Was there something hard that you needed help with? Share the ups and downs of learning to read. We want to hear from you! To get posted on the ABDO Publishing Company Web site, send us e-mail at:

sandcastle@abdopub.com

SandCastle Level: Beginning

Featured Sight Words

again   had

his   me

when   your

Al wants to bat again.

Ben and Jim had
their turns at bat.

Mike wears his
baseball glove.

Grandpa helps me
learn how to pitch.

Kate runs when she
hits the ball.

Your sister Pam is on the winning team.

It's Your Turn to Play Ball!

Juan waits for his turn.

He bats after me.

It is your turn next.

Nick will be up
when you are done.

Juan, Lisa, Nick, and I each had a turn.

We will play again.

More Sight Words in This Book

a	he	the
after	how	their
and	I	to
are	is	up
at	it	we
be	on	will
for	she	you

All words identified as sight words in this book are from Edward Bernard Fry's "First Hundred Instant Sight Words."

Picture Index

ball, pp. 13, 16

baseball glove, p. 9

bat, pp. 5, 7, 20

pitch, p. 11

runs, p. 13

team, p. 15

About SandCastle™

A professional team of educators, reading specialists, and content developers created the SandCastle™ series to support young readers as they develop reading skills and strategies and increase their general knowledge. The SandCastle™ series has four levels that correspond to early literacy development in young children. The levels are provided to help teachers and parents select the appropriate books for young readers.

Emerging Readers
(no flags)

Beginning Readers
(1 flag)

Transitional Readers
(2 flags)

Fluent Readers
(3 flags)

These levels are meant only as a guide. All levels are subject to change.

To see a complete list of SandCastle™ books and other nonfiction titles from ABDO Publishing Company, visit **www.abdopub.com** or contact us at:

4940 Viking Drive, Edina, Minnesota 55435 • 1-800-800-1312 • fax: 1-952-831-1632